ALL KINDS OF FAMILIES

FAMILIES THROUGH ADOPTION

ELIZABETH KRAJNIK

PowerKiDS press.

New York

Published in 2021 by The Rosen Publishing Group, Inc.
29 East 21st Street, New York, NY 10010

First Edition

Editor: Michelle Denton
Book Design: Reann Nye

Photo Credits: Cover YAKOBCHUK VIACHESLAV/Shutterstock.com; Series Art Vladislav Noseek/Shutterstock.com; p. 5 Rido/Shutterstock.com; pp. 7, 11 Dmytro Zinkevych/Shutterstock.com; p. 9 CREATISTA/Shutterstock.com; p. 13 © iStock.com/DragonImages; p. 15 fizkes/Shutterstock.com; p. 17 oneinchpunch/Shutterstock.com; p. 19 njgphoto/E+/Getty Images; p. 21 New Africa/Shutterstock.com.

Cataloging-in-Publication Data

Names: Krajnik, Elizabeth.
Title: Families through adoption / Elizabeth Krajnik.
Description: New York : PowerKids Press, 2021. | Series: All kinds of families | Includes glossary and index.
Identifiers: ISBN 9781725317697 (pbk.) | ISBN 9781725317710 (library bound) | ISBN 9781725317703 (6pack)
Subjects: LCSH: Adoption--Juvenile literature.) | Families--Juvenile literature.
Classification: LCC HV875.K728 2021 | DD 362.734--dc23

Manufactured in the United States of America

CONTENTS

A REAL FAMILY

Families come in different shapes and sizes. Some families have a mom, a dad, and a child or children. Other families are made up of different amounts of parents and children. Sometimes, a child in the family might be adopted. Children are adopted into loving families all the time. Even if a child is adopted, their family is still a real one no matter what.

Families adopt children for many reasons. No matter the reason, the child's adoptive family wants them very much.

About 2 percent of children in the United States are adopted.

WHY PEOPLE ADOPT

People may choose to adopt a child for a number of reasons. Sometimes, a family or person **medically** isn't able to have children. Other times, a person might not want to have children because they may pass on a **disease** to their child. If a woman is in poor health, she may choose to adopt to avoid further health problems.

Some people choose to adopt a child because they want to give them a loving family they might not otherwise have. Other people choose to adopt because they can't have a child alone for some reason.

Some people choose to adopt children on their own. Families with a single parent are just as real as families with two parents.

ADOPTING FROM THE FOSTER CARE SYSTEM

In the United States, the foster care system provides children with a **temporary** caregiver when their birth parents can't care for them. These foster parents have to take classes to learn how to be good caregivers and are **certified** by the state they live in.

Children may end up in the foster care system because their parent or parents have died. Sometimes, the government removes children from their birth parents because they're being **abused**. Other times, children go into foster care because their parent is in prison.

About 59 percent of children adopted in the United States are adopted from the foster care system.

The goal of the foster care system is to return the child to their birth parents once they're better able to care for the child. However, sometimes the birth parent never gets to this point. In cases where the birth parents give up their parental rights, children can be adopted from the foster care system.

Sometimes, foster parents choose to adopt their foster child. This kind of adoption is called fost-adopt. Other times, people who aren't foster parents adopt children from the foster care system.

In the United States, there are more boys than girls in foster care. Most are six years old or older. Many are African American.

ADOPTING FROM ANOTHER COUNTRY

Sometimes, people choose to adopt a child from another country. This happens for several reasons. At times, adopting a child from another country is quicker and costs less money than adopting a child from the United States. Sometimes, the opposite is true.

Some people want to adopt children from other countries because conditions there may be worse than in the United States. Children waiting to be adopted might not have clean water, a safe place to stay, or the chance to go to school. These conditions aren't as much of an issue in the United States.

About 26 percent of adopted children in the United States are from other countries.

ADOPTING STEPCHILDREN

In the United States, it's very common for stepparents to adopt their **partner's** children. In fact, it's the most common form of adoption. Sometimes both parents have children from other **relationships**. In that case, sometimes both parents adopt their partner's children.

For a stepparent adoption to happen, one of a child's birth parents must give up their parental rights. For example, if a father were to get remarried and his new wife wanted to adopt his children, the children's birth mother would have to give up her parental rights for that to happen.

Today, some stepchildren ask their stepparent to adopt them with a card or a surprise. Other times, stepparents will surprise their stepchildren by asking to adopt them.

OPEN OR CLOSED?

A closed adoption is when no **information** is shared between birth parents and adoptive parents. They've never met and have no way of getting in touch with each other. The only information the adoptive family gets is the birth mother's medical history.

An open adoption is when the birth parents and adoptive parents can share information with each other. Birth parents and adoptive parents may keep in touch with emails, phone calls, or meetings. The amount of information they share is different in each family.

In an open adoption, the child's birth mother may choose the adoptive parents. Sometimes the birth mother may allow the adoptive parents to be there when she gives birth.

RUNNING INTO PROBLEMS

Adopting a child isn't easy. It often costs a lot and may take a long time. Sometimes, when there's an open adoption, the birth parent may change their mind about giving up their parental rights.

Some adoptive parents worry about bonding with their child. Children who are adopted later in life may have **behavioral** issues, which can be hard to deal with. If a child is adopted from another country, the adoptive parents may worry about the child's health.

Even though adoption can be hard, it's many people's dream to start a family this way.

Adoptive parents don't face all the challenges of adoption. Adopted children may have a hard time finding their place in the family. This might be more likely if the child feels different from their family or others around them.

Some adopted children have a hard time bonding with their adoptive family. Even if a child was adopted at birth, they may have a lot of feelings about being adopted when they get older. However, every person is different and has had a different life.

It can be hard for adopted children to speak about their feelings with their adoptive parents. Many adopted children go to **therapy** to work through their feelings.

A FAMILY LIKE ANY OTHER

Families through adoption are just like other families. They have parents and children. These families wake up and eat breakfast, go grocery shopping, and have movie nights. Adoption is an event in someone's life. It affects who they are, but it isn't their whole **identity**.

When a family adopts a child, they're choosing to give that child a better life, to love them, and to be there for them. If you have questions about adoption and how it works, even if no one in your family is adopted, you can talk to a trusted adult.

GLOSSARY

abuse: To treat in a cruel or harmful way.

behavioral: Relating to the way a person acts.

certify: To officially say that someone has met certain standards or requirements.

disease: A sickness.

identity: The qualities, beliefs, etc., that make a particular person or group different from others.

information: Knowledge or facts about something.

medical: Of or relating to the treatment of diseases and injuries.

partner: A person someone is in a relationship with.

relationship: The way in which two or more people are connected.

temporary: Continuing for a limited amount of time.

therapy: A way of dealing with problems that makes people's bodies and minds feel better.

INDEX

WEBSITES

Due to the changing nature of Internet links, PowerKids Press has developed an online list of websites related to the subject of this book. This site is updated regularly. Please use this link to access the list: www.powerkidslinks.com/akof/adoption